Trigger Me

Following Fear into Liberation

Dr. Robin L. Colwell

1

For Mum and Dad

Contents

Introduction

The best thing that can happen to us is to be confronted with the object of our greatest fears. This is the cure and the vaccine, the gateway to another world. The moonshot, the bullseye, the lifeline to waking reality. We can't wake up by our own exertion. But when a situation triggers us so utterly, strikes our fears and worries dead centre, and sets our minds reeling in disbelief, our comfort zone is stripped away. The discomfort *must be*. The discomfort is the proof that you are waking up, the physiological evidence, the printed receipt that you are moving away from the sleeping death of untruth. This is when you allow the training you will learn in this book to take over. Prepared, you do nothing but accept the triggering with earnest gratitude. As waves of panic, fear and fury roll through you, close your eyes and curl up the corners of your mouth. When you open your eyes again, you will emerge into the light of what is real and what is good; you will have changed worlds.

You only think you're free

Who among us is not stuck? Immediately, one thinks of the more tangible, obvious ways in which one may be stuck: in an unfulfilling job, an airless relationship, crippled with debt and endless bills, burdened with family, cultural and societal expectations.

However, our usual process is to tackle these outward manifestations of 'stuckness' without attention to or even awareness of the processes that generated them in the first place; we change jobs, relationships, try to make more money, engage in secret pursuits, and seek entertainment. We get temporary hope and relief, or at least distraction. But the processes that got us where we are are intact, and now even more ingrained. And so we continue, enslaved to our behavioural tendencies, unconsciously obeying habits, until any spark of freedom, joy and individuality is buried under cares and problems.

So far, these thoughts are nothing new. They lead to the age-old question of how does one change oneself? And can one change oneself? Of course, this question has been approached from almost every angle, through religion and philosophy, through exercise, diet, and drugs in infinite combinations and permutations. All these meet with occasional success, if one believes the teller or the advertising. More often, though, despite short-lived attempts, most people become more and more fastened to their identities, who they think they are—serving unconscious fears and habits—and their experience of life is increasingly constrained and tight.

This happened to me—my life became smaller and smaller, until one day there wasn't even enough room for me in it. It became so small that all of a sudden I was outside of it. My experience was so steep that its features came into sharp relief, so that I can describe them.

I think that I was, and am, subject to the same forces that act on all of us, but whereas 'being outside oneself' is often a process with an insidious onset and progression, following slow, almost still currents in our unconscious, for me unconscious contents frothed and cascaded out. My hope is that this rambunctious manifestation in me of universal human processes, like a poker player accidentally tipping her hand, has led to sufficient insight to allow me to show you their presence.

What has been the one constant in your life? The one thing that has always been there, through all events, decisions, crises, successes? The answer is *you*. *You* have always been there. And what is the practical means by which you respond to new situations and forge new paths? It is your *will*—the part of you which decides what to do and does it. Your will, your combined faculty of decision-making and doing, is what has been blazing a trail throughout the span of your conscious existence.

Innately, and because we have no reason to suppose otherwise, we assume that this will that we exercise is pure and independent. When we make a decision, we really feel that *we* are making it. We feel that our decisions, or actions, constitute true representations of who we are and what we truly want. I submit that this assumption is a fatal error, and leads to worlds and lifetimes of suffering and separation from true *living*.

What I would like to propose to you is the idea that your decisions and actions only *feel* like yours. Sometimes, perhaps they are really yours. However—and I will unpack this in coming sections—they are usually expressions of habit. And habitual behaviours are often extended coping mechanisms that have developed around an original fear. Even seemingly innocuous 'preferences' (ie choice of restaurant, choice of which street to walk down) may also be downstream behaviours stemming from unconscious or conscious fears. From benign daily habits through to addictions, this is avoidant behaviour, and although it masquerades as free choice, it isn't. Fear has hijacked your will and is forcing you to 'choose' dining at restaurant B or walking down street A.

Returning to the idea of 'stuckness': being stuck is where you end up when your will, corrupted by fear and habit, has made years and years of choices on your behalf. You end up in professional and personal situations that you wouldn't ever have chosen by your own *free*, pure choice. And of course, your true self recognizes the dissonance between itself and your situation. A dim awareness of this causes frustration, anger, more escapism, and can, most tragically, lead to giving up. This dissonance can lead to lurching, violent actions—quitting jobs, initiating break-ups—to attempt to find happiness. The job goes down, the relationship ends—which may be fine outcomes in themselves—but the polluted processes of decision-making are untouched; in fact they are strengthened, and go on to set up new dissonant scenarios: another unfulfilling job, another unhealthy relationship.

And all the while, where were you? Were you observing, participating, weighing, deciding? No. If you haven't identified the fearful tendencies and avoidant habits that are making decisions for you, you are not only not living your life, you're not even watching it! In the dark about what is motivating your behaviour, tricked into thinking that your choices are yours, is it any wonder that your true self is in despair? It should be! You are barely present in your own life. The presence that you do have is dark, still, and stifled. But the good news is that now you know it, and things are about to change. Now you have noticed your 'stuckness,' it's time to start making adjustments.

Loss of Narrative

Right now, *you* are a point of consciousness, a point of attention, reading these words. What are you, exactly? Let's start with what you're doing. Your eyes are scanning these marks, and although they are really just marks on a page, they are being converted by your mind to words, and the words to thoughts. The thoughts are, at least for a brief time, being held and evaluated by you, by your consciousness. Where are they? What realm do they occupy? Your brain, you might say. If we cut up your brain and look at it under a microscope, will we find these thoughts? These words? No… we will find a soggy grey mass, constituted of neurons, in turn constituted of molecules, atoms, sub-atomic particles, and according to the latest science, clouds of probabilities. So where *are* these thoughts? What plane do they inhabit? These thoughts, my thoughts, have seemingly been generated in my mind, for whatever reason, and have, for whatever reason, found it necessary to travel down to my fingers, through a keyboard, where they touch down as words on a screen before leaping into your eyes and mind.

This place, where thoughts pass like traffic on the street, could, for example, be called your consciousness. Apparently dependent on the biology of your body, nutrition, oxygen, etc., tinted or warped by mood, reformulated by intoxicants, reformatted by sleep, consciousness comprises your entire experience of being. However, we don't often even think of it, let alone properly attribute to it its prime importance.

Why should we? What is the purpose of identifying and considering this seat of self, our consciousness? (And as an aside, consider now the amazing fact that consciousness can consider itself. In fact, it can consider the fact that that it is considering the fact that it is considering itself! Consider that fact...) In short, we should develop this awareness because being conscious of consciousness can set you free. It can set you free, irrespective of your particular set of problems. A short list of afflictions from which you can become free would include anxiety, anger issues, sorrow, fears, obsessions, compulsions, addictions, hatred, lusts, and—perhaps most importantly—patterned behaviour.

Think of how much effort we put into behavioural change. We worry about our weight and are anxious about our smoking habit so we diet and try to quit smoking. We try time after time to do it the hard way, and usually fail. By accessing this witnessing self, and turning consciousness on consciousness, we can dissolve the blockages and encrusted habits that are causing the behavior; it's likely that positive lifestyle changes will come, and the process is almost effortless. This is not flippancy—this deep approach is more real than the others: its currency is insight, rather than strict and unguided self-curtailment.

We don't realize how plastic and malleable the self is, and how the heavy encrustations of habit and fear determine identity. Imagine the airy lightness of your consciousness as a baby with pure openness and unqualified experience, and see how the intrusions of the world into that realm began to weigh it down and restrict it. Discomfort, limits of the physical body, fears of abandonment, projected and groundless worries, inherited fears and phobias, compounded together, become the various concerns of adulthood. Behaviours form in response to conscious and unconscious fears, then become cemented in place by habit and repetition. Thoughts, attitudes, posture, tone of voice, movements, gait, plus lifestyle habits encrust and harden. How we show up in the world becomes a conglomeration of our fears, enlivened in part by desires, but both have roots deep in the unconscious, and thus who we think we are actually removes us from true experience.

So when we find ourselves stuck in our frozen palace of fear and habit, how do we get out? Well, first of all, you can't think yourself out of patterned behaviour, but you can be unthought out of it. Here we are, locked in a discursive narrative stream—a train of concepts and words that we are trying to escape from. And how do we usually try to escape from concepts and words? With concepts and words! This doesn't work, although some kinds of words—hopefully these—can prepare the ground for a change in approach. Even 'approach' is too conceptual since it is a formal idea, a stratagem, a plan. As long as a conceptual plan is contained in and tolerable to the wholeness of your being, it can't work. Is it possible to do something so new, so different, that it shakes foundations of your being that you didn't even know existed? You know how people say, when a major event happens in their life—birth of a first child, loss of a parent—that they come home and the room looks different? Well, the ideas we need are the ones that change how the room looks. What I'm pointing to here needs to change your being—your whole being, not certain behaviours that exist as a part of your current being. That doesn't mean that you'll become unrecognizable—no, you'll be more recognizable as yourself when you slough off the accretions of habit and fear. You need to feel your world reel and swim as your frame of reference shifts. And while this shift is by definition out of your comfort zone, the change doesn't have to be uncomfortable. It is only as uncomfortable as you make it by clinging to the interior of your ice palace. When you inhabit a state of 'emergence', where you participate in an unfolding of events, and the events participate in an unfolding of you, then there is nothing for habits and fears to hold on to, and therefore they cannot influence your behaviour. To be a part of this unfolding, to live 'emergently', is to be joined to all that is. Fears, lusts, addictions, and anger need you to have a self, an ego, an identity for them to cling to. When you emerge into genuine presence, you merge with all that is, and they cannot find you.

Look at that last paragraph. How many words, how many ideas, and concepts, does it contain? Those too, while perhaps true in that context, are still words! Still concepts! Look at them, rattling around your brain, pulling you away from palpable, present reality even as they try to pull you closer! And these last words, also! Can you travel back in time to when you knew no words? You were alive then! Then you learned words, and then you learned concepts. Then you began to think, and whereas before it was you *in* the world, now it is you *and* the world. The endless river of your thoughts separates you from the far shore, where you long to be.

Anyway, while I'm not sure that you can just go out there and be more conscious, there do seem to be a few changes of attitude which go along with improvements to one's state of being. Among them would be an attitude of tending in the direction of things one used to avoid. It makes sense to take opportunities to cultivate this change of attitude. When fears are confronted, especially deep ones, this is sure to have an effect on your state of being. But this does not necessarily mean that it is effective to go and seek the things you fear so that you may confront them. I think that this approach is too much of an 'approach', too much of a 'doing'. The whole mentality of 'doing' rather than 'being' or 'participating in' is one that, by the act, sets up a separateness of self that is counter to the integration of self with 'what is'.

Another attitude that goes along with the improved state we seek is *releasing*, and that might well include control of the narrative of our lives. We are stuck in a narrative, our own story, and we fight to make the world fit into it. We become quite upset when the world doesn't perform according to the narrative we have for it. How can we expect to experience the world when we are constantly trying to beat it into the shape we decide it should take? Surely we would prefer to experience the world directly, without the distorting lens of concepts and words—therefore, isn't it most unhelpful to attempt to enforce a narrative of any kind? This fighting, resisting, controlling, running commentary that we inflict on the world—but mostly on ourselves—is not only unhelpful but is a very significant barrier to being alive and awake to *what is*. Ideally, the narrative would stop—loss of narrative—and we would experience the world directly, without the state of remove that is a pre-requisite for commentary. The state of participation in *what is* does not seem to feature any separate viewing gallery from which to observe and comment. When you experience the world with loss of narrative, it is without the interlocutor of an opinionated ego assessing and appraising, packaging and labelling experience until it is thoroughly musty and dead.

Except!! The narration, the separation, the deadness, the fears and habits, as well as the miraculous transformation into freedom and life—how do we know that they do not all constitute the unalterable fabric of *what is*?? The suffering, the insights, the breakthroughs, the slumps into routine and boredom, the deepening tincture of wisdom… all are elements of the unfolding, emerging, *what is*. So what can you do? Possibly, nothing! Possibly not-nothing! But this doesn't have to be bad or hopeless news. Imagine characters in a film. When film is running through the projector, the actors are going to do what is on the film, in the next frames. Imagine a film character who tries to decide what happens in the next frames… he cannot leave the fabric of their existence—the two-dimensional celluloid—and try to effect a different outcome. In the same way, it may be futile for us to fight the unfolding of *what is*. Whatever resistance we do have to *what is*, is, amusingly, part of *what is*! This boils down to the question of whether or not we have free will. I don't know the answer to that, and perhaps no one does. The only sense I have of it is that for me to give you any kind of instructions, on anything, so that you may 'go and improve your life' would not be really how things work. Perhaps it is the case that these words, transmitted from one point of consciousness —me—to another point of consciousness—you—may in some way participate in your unfolding, and I hope that your unfolding may be happy indeed. My guess is, though, that neither I nor you

really exist separately, that there is a glorious unfolding happening everywhere you can think, that all our consternations and joys are a part of it, and what really is happening here is what is happening here.

Trigger me

I suggest that we are to an important degree controlled by unconscious tendencies and ingrained behavioural preferences. These dynamics take over our 'free' will and fashion our lives without our genuine input. Now of course, it would be optimal to become aware of the specifics of our fears and other unconscious motivators. The catch is that any attempts to discover our hang-ups, and be free of them, are governed by... the will. And, as discussed, the will is corrupted and therefore it's hard for it to explore itself. It's not impossible, but I suspect it's slow going and would involve a lot of specific discussion and traditional psychotherapy.

There is available, however, a more powerful, more immediate, and more unpredictable catalyst, through the agency of which one can achieve awareness and presence. It is... other people.

Other people are not subject to your compromised will. They know nothing of your fears, and if they did, may not care about them. This is a great blessing. Simply being around others will inadvertently provoke and trigger you. Other people, in our interactions with them, will comb our psyches and find the weak and tender points hidden to us. These are gifts.

The people and events and things that annoy us the most have the capacity to be wonderful, generous gifts. This is a radical statement. It requires some discerning. Not every noxious thing done to us should be accepted with open arms. There is still a role for our objections to bad behaviour, and of course self-defence in situations where others truly wish us harm. However, these instances are the exception rather than the rule. The majority of behaviours in others which provoke an undue emotional reaction in us are indispensable clues as to what it is deep down that we are truly afraid of. When we are seeking to identify and confront our dark and hidden fears, a faster and more effective strategy than mining our own minds is to gauge and process our reactions to other peoples' provoking and triggering actions.

One of the consequences of fear-based, avoidant behaviour is that we willingly restrict and curtail our experience of the world in order to avoid the objects of our fears. As such, imperceptibly, our lives become limited—our experience of life becomes limited. This is because our compromised will has been setting up the limits and structure of our life. The real you, deep down, knows that life should be bigger and airier than this. That conviction—that deep-seated knowledge that living should feel more alive than it does now—is worth uncovering and holding on to. That feeling will be your motivator for setting up a new and fairly radical way of doing business. And although these new perspectives are radical, they are no more radical than any other repairs or corrections. One identifies what isn't working and replaces it with something that does work. It's no more radical than that.

This doesn't mean that you deliberately have to seek out provoking or triggering situations. It's more about being watchful and waiting for circumstances that ignite emotions—anger, irritation, resentment—and then being open to what these tempests teach you about the weather patterns of your mind.

Consider that your will has constructed a life for you where the things you fear are out of sight. They are not removed; rather, they are in the closets, attic or basement of your mind. They are still in the house. You are 'protected' from them, even though the protection effectively ends your real and present experience of life. So what is actually being provoked and triggered? It isn't *you*, in any genuine sense. It is your comfort zone that has been assailed.

Your safe space is punctured. The closets, attic and basement rooms are wide open again. This is a good thing! The odds that you would have discovered what is so provoking to you on your own are small, because no matter how hard you try, the will, or ego, is always looking to protect itself, wants always to avoid serious puncture and rupture of itself. The more we *try* to break out of our comfort zone, the more solid and intense the sense of a self in need of protection becomes, and the more stuck we become. It is like having your car stuck in the mud—hitting the gas and spinning the wheels fast just makes things worse. This is why events that happen *despite* our will, instead of as a result of it, are such a blessing—they trip us and trigger us, throwing us outside our comfort zone in a way which we could not have achieved by our own efforts.

So here is what happens:

- something provoking happens
- you become upset
- you feel very uncomfortable
- you seek comfort

Here is what can happen:

- something provoking happens
- you become upset
- you feel very uncomfortable
- you accept the discomfort, hold yourself in it, dwell in it, and allow it to stay for as long as it would like

This is not a mere exercise. This is a reality-altering challenge to the forces that imprison you. What happens after this? Afterwards, the world looks different, and you feel more free, and more alive.

Unless you are already are in tune with yourself and living in harmony with who you deeply are, such challenges—triggers—are precious new gifts and are a fast track to becoming who you need to be. The storms of anxiety and worry are now like shells or polished glass that you pick up as you walk on a beach; you hold them and admire them. As you don't want to carry them forever, you eventually put them down again, but gently, and with respect for their beauty.

The spoken or unspoken input of others—not only in terms of how they can provoke and trigger, but also their perspectives and opinions—can be valuable stabilizing information. By this I mean that others provide you with bridging to a broader context: one that isn't so coloured by your particular fears, patterns, and hangups. Of course, other people have their own issues, but, in general, they can help bring you out of your echo chamber and into a freer conception of the world and society.

Empire of Fear

As you turn towards your fears, not only will they lose their power, but they will explain themselves to you. They come into the light. However, this only occurs if you face them directly. This requires some quietness, some resolve, some sensitivity, and some courage. They have been hiding so well, for so long. How do we find them?

This is how:

When things scare you, frustrate you, anger you, do not act. Be quiet, be still. Do not react. Observe what it is that is particularly good at disturbing the stillness of your mind. Feel it in your mind, the presence of vague fear or anxiety. Calmly turn your mind directly into it. Observe what, or who, in your environment, causes you to tense up and tighten. Acknowledge these outer and inner phenomena but do not react. Take mental note of them, breathe, and remain where you are in your body and mind, without reacting.

Normally, these stimuli, or the fear of them, would govern your whole program: what you do and how you do it. It is possible to spend our whole lives in unconscious avoidance of unnamed fears. But now we're going on the hunt. You will find that directly facing these fears is transformative beyond description.

How many years, how many decades, have you been a mindless slave to fear? And if you think you haven't, if your automatic reaction is to reject that idea, ask yourself who is doing the rejecting? If you truly were placid and free of fear, why the rush to discredit this theory? That's the fear protecting itself. We fight so hard to protect ourselves that we also protect our tormentor. But let's not do that anymore. Let's *be* ourselves, in the way that we choose to be.

It may sound a bit facile to tell you to just face your fears. And also, how do you face your fears if you don't know what they are? Let me describe what I'm suggesting a little better. I'm advising the cultivation of stillness and awareness, so that when fears edge in during your life and in your interaction with others, you are more able to perceive them. If the root cause is not apparent, simply turn your attention towards the disquiet and edginess, instead of fleeing it with distracting activities. If you continue to turn towards it and seek its source, it will definitely lose its power and likely also reveal its origin.

Once stillness and awareness become habit, you may have acquired some confidence and want to actually *do* something that your fear tells you to avoid. Actually going directly against fear and doing things you have spent your life avoiding has real explosive power to free you from the concrete tombs of avoidant and patterned behaviour.

Choosing what to actually *do* to challenge your fears takes a light touch and a little inspiration. It could be calamitous, clumsy, and counter-productive if you try too hard. The action of challenging fear might be too direct, too self-driven, too much something *you are doing.* Furthermore, the action of challenging is driven by desire to be free of fear, and desire is something you are trying to get away from because it engages the corrupted will. When you try to get away from fear, too—fear of being a slave to fear—and make a direct pursuit of freedom from fear, it won't work. Rather than mounting an exhausting daily offensive against fear, or trying to force yourself into facing specific fears, I advocate cultivation of stillness and discernment to manage the flow of troublesome thoughts. You are as brave as you are; you can't screw yourself up to a higher level of bravery. And the thought that bravery is what is needed is misguided anyway. What's the point of beating a drum and going to war against something that's trying to help you? A deeper understanding will reveal that your fears are indeed helpful and needed. Quiet attention and discernment will help you know when you can, in the course of your daily affairs, move towards the source of the fears, and when the timing for such movement isn't right.

The cultivation of stillness and awareness is subtle work, but when it happens the right way, the effect is more powerful than whatever could have been accomplished by your direct personal efforts.

What then, is our conscious role, if any, in facilitating these challenges to fear and habitual, pattern-guided behaviour? Centrally, it is to get out of our own way. We do this by gently and consistently stopping ourselves—our laborious thudding thinking, our ham-fisted plans, our strategies of combating desire and fear which themselves are constructed of desire and fear. When the habit of non-reaction and non-action becomes consistent, small illuminated paths present themselves—and with great ease and lightness, we flow down them. The things that seemed so hard—in fact, impossible—we are suddenly doing. Well, actually, the universe is doing them and we are observing the events.

It is hard to mobilize ourselves and pull ourselves together into a strategy of dealing with our situation in the universe when we are so stuck in the misperception that we are somehow separate from the universe. Instead of seeing ourselves as separate entities, doing things to the universe and having things done to us by it, we more correctly should see ourselves as manifestations of the universe, outflowings of it and happenings belonging to it. You are not a thing; you are an event.

As you read this, do you feel your mind straining? Do you feel it weighing these words, examining them, sizing them up for accuracy? Deciding whether they will hinder or assist the organism 'you' in achieving your goals? Do you feel the shadow of fear encroaching on you as you worry about whether you're about to believe something that isn't true, or not believe something that is? As your mind focuses and strains, fear drives it from behind, invisibly. But there is a current in you, an air, a notion, a possibility, that can and does revolt against this situation —that unfurrows the brow when confronted by familiar worries, that pivots to face the worry. That suddenly sees the shadows shift, revealing the true orientation of things. That unveils the angels and demons that wrestle in your waking and sleeping hours. That sees there is no option other than to decline the panic of fear and step towards the steady and the good. No option but the invincibility of fearlessness. So just relax into it. Your daily selves are an electric clash of torrents of energy, stricken through with fear and blinded by ignorance, and occasionally or frequently distorted into convulsions of lust. See how that which you most desire and that which you most fear steer and govern your views, your motions, your literal steps. See how the tightness in your body and mind strangles you into nothingness, with nothing left but a lingering glimmer of love and memory, then see that extinguished. The habit of views, unknowing itself a habit, presents your very thoughts to you and convinces you that they indeed are yours. Fear and desire pollute the reality you drink. The habit of habits pollutes it further and cements it in frozen lattices. The arrogance of the personal view distorts it further, and the inherited prejudices of culture bend it further still.

Please be aware of the empire of fear in which we are embedded and frozen. Fears, ancient and new, named and unnamed, existential to mundane, rip through our being every waking and sleeping sub-second. They tighten your shoulders, pressure your speech; they select which words you will say and which thoughts you will think. They choreograph your movements, time your gait and sculpt your posture. Your handshake, your eye contact, your listening, your pauses, your total presence is manufactured from a blueprint of fears.

Fear pervades us. It pervades our culture, our history, our families, our friends. It inscribes itself on and in our bodies, directs the traffic of our thoughts, imprints and forms our minds and therefore utterly determines our futures. I could go on and on about all the nooks and crannies where it hides. Its whole trick is its invisibility; it has no power when it is directly seen, so it finds ingenious ways to conceal itself. It hides in plain view and we still don't see it as we are so habituated to *not* see it. It operates exactly there where conscious attention isn't—in other words, just off centre stage in your mind. The harder you look for it, the easier it is for fear to dodge the searchlight. It doesn't have to try very hard. Our own busy looking helps it to avoid detection. When it is detected, it doesn't remain in focus for very long. Distracted, disheartened, guided astray, we give up the search and fear regains the upper hand. Obedience to fear is how our minds work, and in a moment we slip back into the labyrinth, the ice castle of fear where our restless spirits wander like ghosts, distracted by want, including the want not to want, and including the fear of fear.

What is the lifeline we may grip to be pulled from this swirling abyss? Here's the secret:

Fear needs our permission. It is entirely dependent on us subscribing to it! It is powerless without our participation. And it is our choice whether or not to heed it! Often, the choice has been made, subconsciously, for a very long time, decades, lifetimes, through unconscious adherence to unnamed rules—rules hammered out by fear when we, in weak and vulnerable moments, let it storm. And now fear enslaves our minds.

That knowledge is a good start. Cultivating an attitude where we politely decline fear, like a recovering alcoholic declining a drink, is a worthy aim. It's something we can do in the glowing *now*, renewing moment by moment our non-interest in the obscuring panic of fear. As we calm ourselves and tune in to ourselves, we become aware of where fear is operating in our lives. This is not done through concentrated attention and seeking, but through non-seeking and non-trying. Settling into a state where the apparatus of attention, seeking, and striving gets thrown into neutral makes the landscape come alive. You are like a hunter in a blind, your senses attuned to the rustling of leaves, the play of shadows, the jingling stream of sound from a stream of water.

The natural sidekick of fear is avoidance. So while it's a great start for you to begin to be aware of the tendrils of fear infiltrating everything, including the mind aware of being aware of fear, this is just a start. Avoidance, the behavioral consequence and effluent of fear, has become the substance of our life, the very material of it. Avoidance doesn't affect our choices—it constitutes, and *is* our choices. With the wellspring of the present moment (which is from birth to death our everything) poisoned and warped by worry, fear and terror, the products of our being in the present moment, our thoughts, words, and actions, all to some degree are avoidant.

Let me ask you this: Without fear, what is it that you need to avoid?

What will you do with this unpoisoned present moment? Acts of love? Of understanding? Of quiet gratitude? Or just dwell in a simple awareness of your own intelligence, sensitively keyed into the present and illuminated by a love that is not so much yours, but rather a love in which you participate?

Who you are and what you do now may be up to you, or it may be up to a, or the, divine presence, working through you. But who you are and what you do are no longer in the realm of fear, no longer subject to that which breathes fear. The Empire of Fear has a new and invincible enemy—you.

You have never seen your hand

What comprises you, in the present moment? Are you sitting? You feel your body, perhaps some discomfort here and there. Perhaps some tension. Perhaps some vague bodily sensations—hunger, thirst, fatigue. These are part of what it means to be you. What else is there? Some less conscious features of you-ness: how you move (briskly? smoothly? jerkily? fluidly?), how you stand, the position of your shoulders, the erectness of your spine. What governs these? Are you instructing your shoulders and spine as to their position? Not usually, right?

How do you pick up objects? How do you place them down? If you take a jacket off a coathanger, how exactly do you do it? Do you use one hand, or two? Do you do it quickly, so that the coathanger clatters about, or in a more smooth and controlled manner? My point is, there are myriad examples of your body language—expressions of who you really are—and often they are more revealing than your words. Although your words are expressions of this subconscious you—in their tone, force, speed and volume—the words that you choose to communicate with provide only a small window into what is in the forefront of your conscious thinking; your body, and body language, paint a much richer picture of who you really are.

Why is body language relevant to what I'm getting at? Well, for one thing, simply noticing body language will give us a clue as to how unconscious we usually are. Why is this important? Because understanding how unaware we normally are can change our behavior quite radically.

If we are so chronically unaware of our physical body, our movements, postures and tones of speaking, why do we make the radical assumption that we know what is going on in our own minds?

The mind, with its vast stores of memories and trillions of nerve connections, is the least understood and perhaps most complicated entity in the universe. And simply because we are aware of a simple plodding train of thought ('here I am and this is what I am thinking of right now') we imagine that we are somehow in command of the whole works, that we more or less know what's going on, although we might grant that there is the odd nook and cranny of our subconscious that we haven't quite got around to checking out yet.

What about taking a more intellectually honest, and less careeningly arrogant view? Namely, that we find ourselves somewhat bewildered on this island of consciousness in a sea of experience, and that we really don't know much more than that?

I think that is a wonderful place to start. And instead of leaping off from this place, let's dwell here a while. Anxious? Dwell there. Scared? Dwell there. Bored? Dwell there. Notice your breathing. Dwell. This room, this place where you think, where you perceive the world, is all you'll ever have. Why not get to know it? Check out the furniture. Here are some insecurities—pick them up. Look at them. Put them down. Here are some fears—pick them up. Look at them. Put them down. Here are some desires. Pick them up. Look at them. Put them down. Breathe. Feel pain? Pick it up. Look at it. Put it down.

All these features of your inner world—fears, pain, desires, to name a few—do you think they do nothing? Do you think they just sit there? They do not. Do you think you are in control of them? You are not. Do you think you perceive them all, in their number, in their reach? You do not. What makes you think that these features are mild-to-moderately important, easily understandable details that you can deal with and neutralize just as soon as you get around to it? They aren't.

If we need a visual analogy of the self, consciousness is like a small, dim light in a grand, dark palace, the architecture of which represents all the features of our psychologic composition—the fears, worries, desires, and so on. Worse, the dim light of our consciousness doesn't know what it doesn't know—and even if it admits this, it will vastly underestimate the breadth and depth of its ignorance. Worse than that, we are possessed not simply by a quantitative deficiency of understanding, but by an entirely wrong view of *what* is.

Why? Why does it have to be like this? Why is it such a puzzle just to be alive? Why do we consistently, individually and as societies, restrict our views to the simplest arrangement of concepts? Why is it that our minds, which actually are capable of perceiving and holding deeper truths, reduce them to the most blunt, rudimentary approximations of the way things are—icons, symbols, maps—and then think these things are reality itself?

I don't know the answer, but I would guess—my brain would guess—that this is simply how the human brain likes to work. It has to work fast to boil down the raw material of sensory and cognitive input into information that we can use in order to stay alive. It simplifies and restricts the picture so that the human animal can survive and not be constantly overwhelmed with cosmic awareness of the fundamental nature of reality, which perhaps wouldn't always be 'practical'.

Fair or unfair, this seems to be the situation we're in. These are the brains we have to work with. Perhaps it is part of a cosmic plan; perhaps the moist grey organ gets used to working certain ways and doesn't often do things differently. So how do we think our way out of our own brains?

Well, I don't think you can just sit down and do it. You might be able to, but I don't think it happens often; it can't be guaranteed. You might just have to wait. Sometimes when we're feeling really stuck, we can't force ourselves out of that mindset. But if you notice that, acknowledge it, don't fight or flee it, just dwell in it, the world will shift and the feeling change. Maybe it takes a flash of the divine. It kind of feels like that. But it also feels like we have the option: take it or leave it. And I don't want you to miss the opportunity. When conditions line up, through not-doing, there's a brief moment where you can accept the invitation to life and freedom. It's a missable opening.

Actually, your whole life is a missable opening. An invitation which can go unopened and unanswered. Actually, this very moment is a highly missable opening. Are you missing it right now?

Imagine that your life is a video game. Imagine that you are a character in the game and have no fear—really, no fear whatsoever —of anything at all. Imagine that you have no worries or preoccupations. Imagine that your desires are completely optional. You like certain things, but if they don't work out, well, no big deal. What kind of a person are you now? I bet you like that person. I bet you'd like to be that person.

Fearlessness, true fearlessness, is an amazing, blessed state, an amazing gift. When you have no fear and want, you are truly present. You notice every waving bough, every creeping bug. You discern the currents of love and the divine moving and flowing through the scene. You walk like you're floating and your touch is soft and tender. You see the lines around your dad's eyes and you love him. You feel utterly continuous with everything.

While such moments feel conjured up by the divine, I think there are ways we can prepare so that we are open when they come knocking. And it's not that I think that there's anything actually 'to do'; it seems that all we can do is get out of our own way. Not that it really matters what 'I' think, but 'I' don't really believe in self or separateness, so when we prepare the way for this happening, it's more like the happening is preparing the way for itself. In fact, no one is doing anything—I'm not typing this and you're not reading it. The universe, or happening, or manifestations of the ground of being, are doing all. But that is perhaps a semantic point. There does seem to be a valve inside us which, when open, allows the universe to flow more freely in and through us.

So there is a role for instructions, even if they are simply ways for the universe to happen and the branches and patterns of being to fulfill themselves.

Here they are:

Stop.

Stop again.

Stop stopping.

Once you've stopped and stopped and stopped some more, by which I mean dwelling, abiding, accepting, not reacting, not reaching, not fleeing and not hiding, you should probably do it some more. Once stopping-observing-not reacting has become your natural home, your refuge, your new manner of being, you might try looking at your hand and see it for the first time.

What's it like to be here, alive and conscious? I'll bet it's the first time in recent memory. It's tricky for me to remember and present its features to you, but I'll try. It's a bit like remembering a dream, or putting together clues. It's a captivating, arresting feeling that encompasses me and everything else. It's almost, *almost*, visual, but a chair still looks like a chair, a cloud is still a cloud. Everything is different—as am I. And not different as in distorted or altered; rather, reality is more real, more apparent. The scales have fallen from my eyes, and while there is no dance of colour or light, things appear as they really are, or, at any rate, more real than they usually are.

Just feel what it's like for you.

Having access to this state, I think, is profoundly healthy, and being here is likely to render many symptoms of mental discomfort remote, at least temporarily.

The narrative

About a week ago, I was riding in the Tonto National Forest near Phoenix, Arizona. It was an amazing day, with perfect weather conditions, good friends, and spectacular scenery. As we were beginning to ride back to the trailhead, my horse Bandit got pricked by a cactus, which made him panic and run. I fell off, hurt my side, and got a nasty gash in my shin.

Luckily, we were able to catch Bandit and get some of the cactus spines out of him. I managed to get back in the saddle, but I knew that I would need to go to a hospital and get stitches, and that Bandit would need to be checked out by a vet.

As we rode back, with my leg beginning to throb, I was thinking about the 'narrative' of that day. I had really wanted 'the perfect day riding', and until the cactus incident, I almost had it. I had begun to create the narrative of that day when I had the idea to go for the ride. Everything was going really well, the plan, the friends, the horse, until reality took hold of my story and changed it utterly.

Emergency Medical Services picked me up at the parking lot, and as we pulled away, I saw my friends getting smaller in the rectangular windows on the back of the ambulance. Had I broken a rib? Would my wound get infected? Would Bandit be okay? My 'perfect day' was gone, as was my control over the narrative. I had no control over this—I was off-script and powerless.

How much of our day-to-day lives (the only lives we live) are spent inside a planned, forced, managed narrative? Are we really open to the world and its events, or do we try to impose our will, our control, over every minute of our days and on the people in them? Let's start with these questions: How do we react when our narratives are challenged? *What is the difference between living inside a narrative and living narrative-free?* How can you tell when you're in a narrative and when you're not? What does it feel like to switch between narrative and non-narrative living?

There's a lot there to unpack. So what happened to me last weekend, and can I learn from it?

To be concise, though, I feel we become less alive when we get too attached to our narratives. The narrative might be something like 'I am safe' or 'Everything is fine', or perhaps 'I need to feel good'.

An intrusive event or thought threatens the narrative, causing us distress and we respond with increasingly patterned, escapist behavior. Because we insist on returning to an intact narrative, we compulsively attempt to normalize the scene, neutralize the offending event or thought, and return to the comfort and security of the original 'script'.

Most people are like this to some degree, right? We have relatively strong expectations about the way things ought to be and the way they ought to go. We resist and complain when reality deviates from expectation. Why are we like this? It might be that we want professional success, or we want comfort, or we want people to like us, or we want everyone to leave us alone, or we want our parents to see us clearly, or we want our children to go that way not the other way...

We have rigid expectations of what life should be like, and we pursue the fulfillment of these expectations single-mindedly, because this can lead to all kinds of apparent success, social, professional, etcetera. But what happens when our expectations are not met, and we find ourselves outside of our narrative/comfort zone? We are decidedly *not* good at letting go and accepting change. Instead of doing so, we fight to restore our comfort zone, or if we can't, turn to behaviours which at least simulate comfort. Behaviours can start very subtly, with minor choices about how we live our lives, but can become extremely pervasive, to the point that almost every single thing we do is designed to seek and shore up our comfort zone. The result is, of course, that we become imprisoned in this behaviour. We are unable to fully experience life; we are under a 'protective' bell jar, which to some degree protects our expectations, but in a more real sense deadens our experience of life and freedom.

How do we get out?

When I put my horses into their pens for the night, I shut the gate and close the latch. The latch is not a very complicated mechanism, but the horses still can't get out. They may know that freedom is out there on the other side of that gate, but they can't get there, because they don't understand the mechanism that locks them in. Their brains aren't used to thinking like that. Similarly, we are stuck in certain patterns of behavior, and our minds are not used to thinking about the locks and mechanisms that confine us. And while we are unused to that kind of thinking, the modes of thinking that *do* confine us operate ceaselessly. In almost any given moment, including the ones in which we are thinking specifically about these problems, our minds seek comfort and control. This tireless attempt by our minds to define and influence reality is what puts us and keeps us in our behavioural cages.

How then do we take *back* control, when too much control is the problem? How do you use your free will in a healthy way, when your own brain is constantly hijacking it and using it to secure a phony comfort zone?

Furthermore, how do you counter this pattern, for the rest of your life, in all situations, high-stress and low-stress, going against years, perhaps decades, of deeply ingrained coping strategies and unconscious behaviours?

Well, it's not easy. It's a journey into advances and setbacks, slumps and victories. But with new insight, even the setbacks are transformed into progress. It's a lot easier than continuing the same way. The entire landscape will change: whereas before, you were stumbling around in darkness, confusion, and distress, now you can see your enemy and have a clearer view of how it operates. You will almost immediately have a new comprehension of your struggle, a new sense of mastery of your situation (even during setbacks); you will feel less distress, more optimism, and discover more freedom to enjoy life.

Really though, how do we get out?

To free ourselves of from the mind-prisons in which we live—like the horse pens with the latched gates—we need to understand how we got here. For years and years, more or less unconsciously, we have heeded the little voice of fear, and made decisions based on avoidance of anxiety and discomfort. More or less unconsciously, our obedience to the promptings of fear has kept us inside our comfort zone, or 'approved' narrative. As we continue doing this, our comfort zone becomes smaller, and freedom is progressively restricted, until it's basically gone. This state of affairs is no minor problem—it, and the road that leads to it, contain untold misery. So now, armed with this understanding, how do we interrupt this cycle of behavior?

One of the ways this mind-prison gets bricks in its walls is by you buying into a fairly rigid definition of reality: what is good, what is bad, and what are acceptable and unacceptable outcomes. This narrow and rigid brickwork in which we establish our likes and dislikes and make our choices is largely cemented together by fear, and it is here, in the mortar, that avoidant, fearful behaviour sets up shop and thrives. We can take bricks out of the walls of our mind-prison by loosening the mortar, the glue, and breaking up this rigid way of perceiving the world. We need to learn to be less 'grippy' with our lives. When I first noticed the walls around me I was surprised at how much I was imposing my views on the world, and on other people. I hope I'm not still doing it.

When you go through your day, feel how open or closed you are. How much are you insisting on your own narrative? Are you insisting on a narrative right now? Am I? Even when we're focused on learning and trying to become more open, our brains are still operating in the way they usually do—fixating on worries, fears, and seeking ways to avoid them. Those who meditate know how much effort and concentration it takes to be free of the babble of discursive thought, where our thoughts cascade at us in a bewildering jumble. Often, the babble is driven by fear. Can you perceive them now, those scary, intrusive thoughts that trick you into thinking you need to do a certain deed, say certain words, think certain thoughts as a matter of protection? Fear co-opts our autonomic nervous system, making our hearts beat fast, our skin sweat, our bowels churn. In such a state, it's hard for us to dwell in and contemplate the anxiety: instead, once again, we seek (temporary) relief of mind and body.

In general terms, we need to open our minds and become less sure of the correctness of our habitual ways of perceiving the world. I don't think we need to worry about becoming 'space cadets', mainly because we are already so restricted in our perceptions that opening our minds will only bring us a little closer to reality. But even a little closer will give us a healthier way of experiencing the world.

What is reality? You can dive into this question (if you like) from within most religious, philosophical and scientific paradigms. Asking this question will not break with creeds or undermine beliefs. Religious and scientific thinkers, when pursuing the question of reality, tend to come to a place of increased openness and wonder. The closer they approach, the greater the wonder. My purpose in saying this is to make this point: by relaxing our minds into a state of true wonder, we take power away from the threats and abuse of fear. The terrible things that we are afraid of—if they actually happen (which they likely won't)—will not seem so terrible. From a state of openness, is *anything* so dire and terrible?

How then, should we view fears and anxieties? I suggest that they are the clues to our freedom. They are the points of friction, of poor fit, between our created, false reality, and the actual world. Without them, we would be completely lost. Walls or no walls, we wouldn't have any way to get out and get free. So let us begin with gratitude for our fears, as they are going to guide us back to life and freedom; let's pay close attention to them, instead of trying to shut them out. Let's thank them for keeping us safe: they point us where we need to go; they shine a light on the path that leads to freedom.

Truly taking aboard this new way of looking at fear will entirely change your experience. Fear is no longer a curse, but a blessing, a guide; fear will show you the way to happiness. Instead of being constantly engaged in a stressful fight against fears and anxieties, you can seek them out, dwell with them, reflect on them.

Does this mean that you should run around maniacally confronting the things that scare you? I don't think so. That approach is too self-driven, and not characterized by carefully listening to yourself and observing situations. The things that scare us come to us eventually anyway, sooner or later. Pursuing them directly is too effortful. Instead, we can try to live our lives mindfully, following the dreams that we already have, and mentally preparing ourselves to not flee from fear when it inevitably strikes.

So cease frantically trying to avoid anxiety, and just look at your fears with interest and gratitude. Why panic? Everything you fear is an invitation to reality; every worry is a portal to life. As you spend time with the thoughts and situations that you fear, you will gradually—or perhaps rapidly—float up and out of your prison and surface into the world of the living.

It is perhaps not reasonable to expect an immediate and permanent reversal of your condition, but this new perspective *is* a game changer.

Signal milk

Have you ever considered that you exist outside of yourself? That when you give your hand to someone else, it is to them someone *else's* hand? The cast of characters in your mind—your family, your friends—dwell in interior worlds as complete as yours, and in which you play a role as mysterious and separate to them as theirs are to you.

Do you ever think that you do not create the world? That smoke does not rise for you, nor rain fall? That the glowing, throbbing representation of the world that you see through your eyes actually is there when you don't see it? When your eyes are no more, the sun will still shine on the hills, the rain will still soak them, and cool rivulets will run down their creases.

Imagine that world, which will be there after your body dies. Your skin will not feel the warmth of that sun, and your fingers will not feel cool water. That world is still there, right? What is that world, imperceptible to your bodily remains? Is the sun hot when you cannot feel it? Is the water cool? The heat, the coolness, the shadows and colours that your senses perceive now, do they describe the world to you, or do they block your experience of it?

Imagine you are a king or queen in your palace. You have five elderly servants—sight, sound, touch, smell, and taste. Every day they report to you on the beauty of your kingdom and its splendours. But you remain in your palace. One by one, though, as they are elderly, all your servants get ill and pass away. That day, you venture out your palace doors and experience, for the first time, your kingdom. But now you are experiencing it as it is, rather than as it was described. Our senses convey to us signals from reality, but we do not experience reality directly. Our senses have us drinking signal milk and dependent on it; in fact, for as long as our sensations report the world to us, provide us the milk, we are imprisoned in a false sense of the completeness of the report.

And I don't mean that there is some kind of malicious scheme to hide reality from us, and our senses are in on the game. In terms of survival of the body, the senses are obviously very important. They carry into us information from the external world, so that we don't step off a cliff or burn the pizza. But who told you that what your senses don't perceive, doesn't exist? No one, right? It's just a natural kind of assumption to make.

I think it is very desirable to have some direct experience of reality beyond the streams of sensory input. So how do we get there? How do we see past the curtain of what our eyes show us? How do we hear what's on the other side of sounds? How do we touch what isn't there? Fear almost guarantees our non-presence, and its siblings, anxiety and worry, get in on the act. Let us say that you have turned towards fear and are peacefully dwelling in it so it no longer bars you from entry to reality; even as you become free of fear, there is something else in the way—the habit of reckless inattention. As long as it predominates, your experience with reality will be occasional and accidental. Attentive, peaceful attention to the moment, and a gentle, steady redirection of attention away from distractions and emotion is a good start. Once you are not fleeing from fear, but are turned towards it, the walls fear puts up will dissolve. But in order for you to experience what is real, the ground also needs to go. That is your fixed identity, your self, your pride in what you are, your history, accomplishments; in short, your attachments to your story. Can you feel a tiresome, pushy sense of self always insisting on the primacy of its experience? As long as this bully is barging around the scene there can't be much true presence. Flight from fear, absorption in (false) self, distraction from love all wrest us out of the present and obscure what is real. These are like layers of gauze. Constant reliance on the stream of sensory signals deceives us into believing that this is a fulsome account of reality, rather than, at best, shorthand for what is.

As if dependence on signal milk and reckless inattention weren't enough impediments to presence, we also carry around with us the view of the present as the permanent. While intellectually we know this is not true, we think and act for all the world as if it is. We are frozen. We balk at change, or become profoundly destabilized by it; we perceive change as traumatic and beyond our control. But! This destabilization that comes with change is precisely healthy because it disrupts our comfortable sense of permanence. Change dislodges us from the accreted habits of thought and being and sends us into the current of impermanence.

The comfort we take in the illusion of permanence guarantees our separation from reality, and guarantees our suffering when, inevitably, reality makes itself apparent. It is much better to dwell in the knowledge and deep acceptance of impermanence so signs of impermanence are less likely to be disruptive; we will be better able to live a tender life of love and presence.

We also take comfort in the illusion that we each have a separate identity. As a way to get the floor under our feet, we identify with this personhood, these accomplishments; we distinguish ourselves by this feat or action. The word distinguish—to make oneself separate and distinct from one's surroundings—reveals our intent. Why do this? What is the statement you want to make? What is the fear that you want to dissipate? Are you afraid of not being exceptional? This is not a mocking question—I too am afflicted by it and I want to look deeply into my motivations. If these words are not published, and are not validated by others, what will that then mean? I am afraid that I won't have been exceptional. (I am afraid, on a deeper level, that I won't have *been*.) But let us examine this possibility. That I, Dr. Robin L. Colwell, of Saskatchewan, Canada, and you, dear reader, are not at all exceptional. Let us pose that you and I are the picture of the ordinary. What was it we imagined we might do? The rotation of the Earth on its axis is not likely to be affected by anything we might do. But guess what is profoundly affected by our actions? The people, animals, and plants around us. They are not very interested in what great outward feats you and I may achieve, but if we are able to be present, undistracted, sensitive, and most of all, loving, then that has the capacity to turn the axis of their worlds.

I think we can get a glimmer of this through meditation. Meditate on an object, and you may get a faint signal of what it actually is.

Guess what else? We actually do have deep knowledge and deep understanding, as well as deep peace. These bubble up from time to time, but in mental acts of stupidity, insensitivity, foolishness, and carelessness we brush them aside in favour of the milk of our senses and the affairs of the world. And we remain on the run—chased around by our fears and unaware that it is we who give them life. Chased by fears, led around by desire, which usually is powered by fear too, unaware of what we are unaware of, we are needlessly afraid, tragically and self-destructively angry, blind and unconscious, hopelessly ignorant of the contours of the ground upon which we stumble around. Distracted from love, although it radiates through our lives, we rush into dark crannies of worry, fear, and want, and hide. Instinctively, we sense that we at least should pay lip service to love, but we allow it the merest sliver of our attention, and only once our other 'needs' are met. We need to take refuge in love. Anything else is distraction.

The program that's escaped from the program

A little while ago at work, I saw a co-worker that I hadn't seen for a few weeks. She asked me how I was, and I gave a kind of absent answer, a bit of a lame half-joke, along the lines of 'no news is good news' or something like that. She then told me that I had said the same thing last time she had asked how I was. '*Exactly* the same thing?' I asked. And she said, 'Word for word.'

In addition to seeing this as not particularly friendly or present of me, I was chilled to realize, again, that my mind runs in utterly predictable patterns.

Where I live in Saskatchewan, Canada, it is cold in winter and the desolate landscape has more in common than the moon than with the rest of Earth. (I say this with affection—I do like it here, and winter is one of the reasons). This past winter, I was rotating my horses through a training program, which required trailering them to a training barn a four-hour drive from where I live. Two trips, several weeks apart. On the second trip out, with not a soul around, and after hours of driving with nothing but flat white fields from horizon to horizon, I pulled over to pee. I stepped to the margin of the snow-and-gravel road and found myself exactly—EXACTLY —in front of a yellow patch where I had stopped to pee three weeks earlier. I was not off by an inch to the left or the right. The Earth rotates on its axis at 1600 km/hr, orbiting the sun at 30 km/second, and our Milky Way galaxy moves in space at 2.1 million km/hr. Embedded in the reeling cosmos, my mind in just two trips had established a pattern, and determined with 100% accuracy where I was going to pee after several hours at highway speeds through featureless landscape. I know that we don't consciously perceive the Earth's rotation, or movement through space, but my point is that amidst all the movement and fluctuation of life and existence, the mind is shockingly powerful when it comes to subconsciously establishing subtle patterns and habits. It determined where I would stop on my second trip to the training barn, so imagine how firmly and completely it governs the things we do on a daily basis!

While we think that we are free, this is an illusion. We aren't reacting freely to new events. The program of who we are is running and determines what we will do in any new circumstance. Our backgrounds, our fears and wants—which determine our preferences—can almost always entirely predict what we are going to do and say. As we get older, our maps and patterns become bulkier and more absolute; we are 'stuck in our ways'. Some people won't accept an invitation if it is outside of what they normally do. I'm sure you know people like that. People declining invitations think they are making a free choice, because they aren't conscious of the encroachment of habits and fears in their decision-making process. What about you? Are you conscious of the forces and currents that direct your mind? I think it's a safe bet for us to assume that we have only scant knowledge of these forces. I think too that only in direct acknowledgment of our ignorance, do we have a chance of making a free decision. Otherwise, our programs are just running us.

All you need is a glimpse of how programmed and patterned you are to understand the importance of a truly free, original choice. Do you realize that you have been patterned your whole life and have never done a single thing free from the shadow of some fear or worry? Pay attention to this moment. This moment is crucial, as it establishes a new axis, a new dimension of choice and existence. Instead of running around in your usual mazes, mechanically reacting to events according to your predetermined program, ask:

What are the reasons behind why I do what I do? And: *Why am I how I am?* This is incredibly powerful.

Visualize yourself as a program, a computer program. Computer programs are designed to accept certain kinds of input and respond to that input. The response, however, is determined not so much by the input itself as by the way the program is designed to respond to input. The response of the computer program is 100% consistent with the program itself. It can't break out of itself and do something entirely different. If you ask a calculator what three times three is, it can't say that that is obvious and it would prefer to talk about the weather. Slavishly, it issues its response, according to its circuitry. How boring it must be to be the mind of a calculator. But I am afraid that we are very much like this.

If you have the mind of a calculator, running on properties programmed into it, and have no true free choice, what can you do about it?

I would suggest that the first event in becoming free is an acknowledgement, a *prise de conscience*, that we are influenced by factors of which we are unaware. Once acknowledgement is present, go deeper. Relax. It is like perceiving a drift, a current, a fragrance of lilacs in the breeze. This influence can perhaps feel like a subtle tug, or a drifting in a certain direction, away from the hard-walled prison that severely limits any experience of free choice and free life.

How much is affected and determined by our programming? What inputs, cues and tones do we pull in from the environment to constitute the material of our experience? We vastly overestimate our ability to know and account for the factors that influence us. We tend to think of ourselves as aloof from the environment, autonomous, and free. This is so factitious! First of all we are a part of our environment, influenced by it and influencing it. There is no sharp border between our self and not-self. Within our programs, we cannot just zoom out and get the satellite view. We don't know what we don't know. This is why it's so important to be attentive to clues.

What we can do is acknowledge the limited scope of our perception and understanding, and dwell here. *Dwelling* paradoxically widens our scope and allows us to live more fulsomely informed by truth and reality. The decisions made from this posture of mind are better than the automatic output of our programming.

You are a program. We all are. But you are a program that is capable of escaping from its program.

So that's what being me feels like!

It's a curious thing, to live into middle age with no knowledge of what it felt like to be me. That was my case. This is not an exaggeration or a poetic turn of phrase. I believe this describes what actually occurred.

If from an early age we are imbued with fears and preoccupations, habits and wants, these in no time flood the experience of true awareness and aliveness, turning us into automatons of habit and servants of fear. Being liberated from these influences is a profoundly strange experience; it returns you to your seat of awareness and agency which was stolen from you long ago. The feeling of liberation is most real and most direct. You feel the muscular tension around your eyes relax and a new ease of breath. You feel true freedom of choice in your day-to-day activities: you now can fearlessly relax into each moment and enjoy an unpolluted approach to being and action. Whereas previously a day felt like a panicked and fraught obstacle course, now it is open and welcoming.

This is a wonderful gift, to feel how it feels to be you. You are not the fears and worries which have overgrown your mental space and enslaved you both physically and mentally, you are you! The you that was there as a baby and young child, before the world decided that it was more important than you and you were deceived into believing the same.

Karmic completion

Why does it feel good to do something you're afraid of doing?
Why does it feel bad to continue to avoid something you're afraid
of doing? It is interesting to consider these questions. How long
has that fear existed? Perhaps it has been rolling around your mind
for years. Perhaps it's been a drain and an ebb on your soul, a
brake on your freedom, for decades, or your whole life. Perhaps it
has deformed your social life to a tiny, warped fraction of what it
could be.

When you started being afraid of something, tension was created.
When you avoided what you were afraid of, the tension was still
there. It didn't matter where you went, the tension was there, in
that space. The tension was there in your sleep, and in the farthest
corners of the Earth. This is because it lives in your mind—a
tautness, an incompletion, a fault, a separation of you from you.
Finally, it becomes too much. You can believe that you decide to
face your fears, or that angels have been deployed to rescue you,
but it comes to the same thing: you stop running. Let's say you do

that thing that you have feared. See what happens to your body and your nerves. After the initial tightness, the tunnel vision and the anticipation, comes an emotional release, the feeling of being flushed with accomplishment, the settled feeling of mastery and conquest. Relaxed body language, directness of aspect, the fullness of movement—these all follow the event in which fear has been directly faced. You make friends with your fears; you shake their hands and show them love and compassion. Now you promise them that you will take care of them. They are like helpless creatures. You accept them and love them fully. And in this moment, you lose the duality that afflicted you. It is no longer a conflict between you and them; it's just you. You—with your beautiful, hard-earned fears that you embrace as essential parts of you. No matter how big or how small, how terrifying or silly, you invite them into your heart and promise to take care of them.

With each fear you lovingly embrace, a broken hoop in your heart is mended. Each time you take a fear in, you become more whole, more solid. You end up realizing that you may as well take them all in. You may as well do it sooner rather than later. There isn't any point in holding your fears away any longer—you are just prolonging the tension within your fractured self by doing so. Invite them in and become whole.

It may sound strange to love your fears, but here is what I mean: Stop. Feel where your tension is. In your voice? In your body? In your choices? Breathe and accept that tension, that fear. It is there. This is a mental act of non-avoidance. Perceive the fears that have been controlling you from their hiding place, then turn towards them.

We think of fears as noxious, intrusive elements attacking our peace from the outside. But this is not true. They have nothing to do with the outside world. They begin in your mind and persist there. Certain things in the outside world are emblems of this fear, but the wound, the problem, is inside you. Outside of you, the world is just fine. When you approach and face the things in the 'outside world' which you fear, you are actually looking inward to your deep wounds and healing them. The world outside you remains just fine. Once your mind and attention has settled on and healed these trouble spots, you are capable of living in greater continuity and peace with the world. Your relations with humans, animals, and even objects becomes fuller, richer, and you will feel the harmony reaching into each forgotten corner of your life. Conflict dissipates. Deadness and emptiness give way to life and fullness.

Approached this way, our hang-ups, our fears, our flaws, turn into the most beautiful and personal parts of us. Each flaw is a unique portal through which we may access an experience of the way things really are. How flat and uninteresting we would be if we were 'perfect'! We should cherish these beautiful features of ourselves and be grateful for what they can teach us. Through these 'imperfections' we are granted a real, personal experience of revolutionary growth, surpassing what we used to think comprised the limits of experience and guiding us to a new land of richer meaning and fulfillment. Finally, we are not embracing our flaws in order to 'get rid' of them—there is no need; they are our emblems of perfection. Do you think the universe was made in total perfection except for the struggles in your mind? No, your every struggle is a part of magnificent creation, like the rings of Saturn. You are perfect and a wonder of creation. These 'flaws' and 'imperfections' are exactly positioned to guide you to a condition of greater presence and freedom. If pressed to find fault and imperfection, perhaps we might look for it in our uncomprehending, petulant attitude towards these lifelines to reality.

Disappointment

What is disappointment? You thought things were going to be one way, and they were another. What causes anger? You thought things were going to be one way, and they were another. You thought you were going to enjoy a nice walk, but it was interrupted by an unpleasant phone call. You bought this book hoping it was going to fix things and put ground under your feet, but now you feel more uncertain than before. What is fear? You want things to be a certain way, but are worried they might not be. What is hope? You want things to be a certain way. What do all of these concepts have in common? They have in common that you are trying to stick to a storyline, an approved narrative. When you want things to be a certain way, when you prefer or seek this outcome or that development, you are asserting your *self* and the satisfaction of your *self* as the key determinant of 'happiness'. Even when behaving in a way society may deem 'altruistic', the self, and gratification of self, is still very much in the centre. There is little difference between volunteering for a charity and robbing a house. The self has a goal for itself, acts in order to satisfy itself. That does not mean that one should not volunteer for charities, or that one may as well rob a house—it just means that gratifying the self is central to both scenarios. Of course, even trying to be free of self-gratification is nothing other than self-gratification.

I don't think, however, that it is pointless to consider our self-serving patterns of thought and action. This simple insight—that we desperately cling to our preferred narratives and outcomes, often hastily assembled piles of vanities and anxieties—can be breathtakingly healthy. While our *modus operandi* may continue to be, to some degree, self-serving, we at least have a broader view, and are less easily upset by the antagonisms of life. This will lead to a greater degree of freedom: whereas a situation may previously have provoked and angered, it may now provide a departure point for a broader, wiser perspective.

Perhaps this capability is divine. It seems that no other creatures on earth can ask why they want what they want, or why they are thinking what they are thinking. Of course many or most humans don't do this either—but you and I can. Certainly, this insight is useful in almost all spheres of life, and once developed, you will find it appreciated by others.

Usually, to begin this kind of self-interrogation, we need a crisis. We need to be in a bad way and need help of some kind. But how adherent we are to our preferences and narratives, almost to the bitter end! Our perception of ourselves is so bull-headed, we tend to ignore genuinely helpful advice and input. We tend to run our program full-tilt to its completion—smoking until we have cancer, being selfish until we're divorced. For some reason, true caution and circumspection seem always to be earned the hard way.

There is another way. The alternative is to perceive our programmed tendencies and try to avoid the wreck, or at least avoid a big wreck. Or, rather, don't try to avoid, just shift to a more grounded mode of behaviour, take curves at appropriate speeds, stay out of the ditch.

This is a big process and can span years and comprise a multitude of developments (hence aisles upon aisles of self-help books). A key concept in this process, however, is to develop awareness: of how fixedly we pursue our narratives, and of our patterns of response when reality inevitably turns out to have other plans.

Once we gain insight as to our desperate fixation on our storylines, we begin to understand how severely they limit our freedom. Our vigorously defended storylines exist to protect an idea about our identity—a conceptualized version of ourselves which is both highly inaccurate and grossly restricting. It is only accurate insofar as it describes the person we like to think we are. The person we *actually* are is hemmed in and reduced by this partly conscious imposition of a preferred (and fictional) identity. This invisible cage gives us only short-lived comfort: its purpose—to delineate our boundaries in the confusing flood of existence—works only so far. Yes, we choose to pursue certain features of it in order to satisfy our vanities, insecurities, etc. We may choose a certain prestigious career because of insecurity, or a lucrative one because of fear of poverty. But while this identity, this walled fortress against reality, provides a nest of comfort, it is constantly being pulled apart by reality, and the distress of defending and repairing it is exhausting. It is ultimately fatal to believe that you are who you think you are. This is the point of total defeat, and tragically often results in suicide, or capitulation to a life of medical sedation. This is how the imagined identity fails in the real world. It really is a good thing to be rid of. Our fictional identity, and the storylines that we protect to defend it, together constitute the 'program' that we're running, and we think it is the only program that we can run. But there are radically different ways of you being you—you don't have to persist in running a model of you that doesn't work. When the evidence becomes overwhelming that your program isn't working—broken relationships, substance abuse, and unhappiness —it's time to switch programs. Your ability to switch programs will depend on the knowledge that your identity has no firm boundaries, other than those you consciously or unconsciously choose by fear, craving, or sheer habit.

Imagine two invisible, vast oceans: your true self, and reality. The person you think you are, your identity, is just a thin, false line between two invisible floods. Let go of that line.

How was your day?

Are you trying to make your days good? This is a trap. Your days can be good, but not if this is what you seek. Trying to have a good day sets you right up to be pulled around by desires and chased by fears. Instead of trying to have a good day, try to have a real day—one in which you are awake in your heart and your mind.

In such a day as this, there is no strain or worry. You are aimless, with great purpose—the purpose is the aimlessness. This does not mean that you don't do anything. Quite the opposite. Such days will be exceedingly productive. However, achievements are not strived for, but occur as a by-product of focused aimlessness. Instead of taking your fears and desires off the shelf in the morning, as you usually do, to work on them and become frustrated, just leave them there. Remain in the moment, and allow the day to come to you. This does not mean passivity—this approach is highly successful at all levels of activity, even, and especially, in fast-paced physical action. There is always good reason to be present in the moment, but perhaps especially during periods of fast activity.

Do not try to fashion your days, weeks, years, and life. This is a trap, based on the fallacy that anything is more important than the present moment. Dwell in the present moment, improve it with increased receptivity to what is actually occurring, and you will naturally improve your days, weeks, years, and life. Your life isn't a dream, it is real. But as soon as you turn your attention to pursuing desires, or avoiding objects of fear, you are pulled out of the moment; and when you live outside the moment, harried and distracted, you *are* in a dream and are unable to improve the way you relate to reality.

A good day is not a day without pain; a good day is not a day without trouble. Days without pain or trouble are days that do not reflect the reality in which we live. A deferral of, or distraction from, trouble, is not good for us. Goodness is intimate with and inseparable from trouble. Trouble and pain are needed for goodness to reveal its lustre. I know, what we really want is peace and rest, but these are not truly available in their absolute forms while we are alive. What is possible for us, however, is a balanced and deep experience of our condition. Instead of resisting pain and trouble, accept them—not grudgingly and bitterly, but acknowledging pain's presence and trouble's power as essential players in your story. Pain, fear, and trouble are in a deep sense true companions and patient teachers. Our instinct to shun them is what keeps us in the dark and prolongs suffering. If we instead are open to them and to where they would guide us, they will lead us out of suffering, and back to life.

The second camera

Many, possibly all, of our problems occur and persist because we are stuck in ourselves. We find it very difficult to see this because we can't see ourselves plainly and correctly. We can be quite wrong in our ideas about how we are. Other people see traits in us immediately, as soon they witness us walk into a room. And even though these traits may be pervasive and cause us deep problems, we can go an entire lifetime without being conscious of them. How do you show up in a room? What is immediately apparent to the eyes and hearts of those you meet? What is immediately telegraphed to everyone around you by your clothes, your posture, the rapidity or slowness of your movements, your tone, your word choice, your sentence structure, your eyes and how they move or rest? By the content of your speech, by your choice of action? By the type and nature of your re-actions? All of this output, vast and subtle. Any psychologist or observer of people knows that we are terrible at seeing ourselves, the way we are. This does not just apply to the way we appear to others, or to our general presentation to the world. We are even less aware of our patterns of choice and behaviour. Events in the world exert an emotional effect on us, and we are usually ignorant of how our emotions sculpt our thinking and responses to events. This leads to vicious cycles of maladaptive, unconscious behaviour and endless suffering. We don't know why we think what we think. And when we try to think about why we think what we think, we are subject to the limitations of our perspective. In fact, the harder we think about our thinking, the more trapped and narrow our understanding becomes.

So how do we come out of this trap? How do we see ourselves as we are? We don't want to do this out of vanity, or as a kind of superiority mission; we want to relate to the world and live in peace, and wisdom. Of course, even this desire to have a truer idea of ourselves, so that we can live in peace and harmony, is in itself a thought and a desire. So how do we go upstream, to the source of thoughts, when they still are in pixels, ungenerated, unassigned? How do we become aware of the free stirring of thoughts at their very source?

Imagine that your life is a movie. Your surroundings, your actions and their consequences are recorded by the camera of your consciousness. You are seeing and recording the events of your life. Your other senses, your thoughts, experiences, emotions, memories are the primary crew helping to operate this camera filming your life. To observe the filmmaking process (how you think, without thinking), you need a second camera. Try opening up this second camera in your mind, right now. You will be able to watch how you think and how you relate to the world. The second camera, once it is up and running, is far more neutral—hence accurate—than the first one. The second camera is unaffected by prejudice, egotism and the tints of emotion.

One traditional and effective way of setting up this second camera is through meditation. I mean being very still, and stopping each thought as it comes up. In this stillness and space between cancelled thoughts, you remain open and sensitive to currents that are stirring behind thoughts, even as your mind attempts to generate them. Try to do this wordlessly, thoughtlessly: simply, and neutrally decline each thought. It is like walking through a market. As people call to you, hold out goods to you, you politely say no thank you, and walk through the crowd; you have no need for anything here. If you abide in this non-need for the thoughts your brain is trying to sell you, you will begin to notice tendencies and patterns in how you normally buy into thoughts. Does the vendor of angry, bitter thoughts typically try to sell to you when you are working at a job you don't like? Does the stall selling fearful, panicky thoughts bombard you with advertisements when you haven't slept well, or when you are worried about money? These are just examples of the myriad interplaying currents and influences which produce the experience of being you. By calmly declining each thought, you create a space in which the experience of being you is not constantly slammed around and distracted by discursive thoughts generated amidst the weather systems of emotion. This second camera, this inner witness, is removed from the broiling elements of your psyche, but it is delicate and evanescent. As soon as it begins to record distinct thoughts, words, and images, it is merely copying the main camera. In other words, as soon as you feel that you have gained perspective, you have lost perspective. The initial inkling of the second camera perspective is correct—you register a shift, a newness, a freshness of view—but when it hardens into a distinct thought (and even words), you return to your habitual manner of thinking and being. This is just the mind operating in its usual manner, because that is what it is accustomed to. And, sorry to say, even this is conceptualization, thinking, orientation of the ego to a particular view; ultimately all conceptualization is invalid and dispersed by its own logic. The idea that a view must undercut itself and implode to be valid, itself is undercut and imploded, without limit. To skirt this process is a non-process, conceptlessness, a non-conceived, non-verbalized, unredacted experience of reality. Now, forget the cameras. Every thought about holding a leaf in your hand removes you from the truth of holding a leaf in your hand.

Nothing in this perplexing scheme, however, excludes the real phenomenon of insight. Insight is always wordless: the mind moves, and the landscape previously known to it in the baking monochromatic glare of habitual thought is now thrown into relief and texture by the crisp, long shadows of insight. A comparison of what was thought to be true before insight and what is known to be true now *can* be put into thoughts and words. There is an urge to describe the now more precise contours of existence. This paragraph is an example: these words describe an insight; they traverse and map the contour of an idea. What I'm trying to describe with these words is that insight is not a *de novo* creation, or even a creation at all. An insight happens when your mind moves and *knows* things from a new perspective; it doesn't *create* the new perspective. But positions and perspectives are limitless; and being stuck in one perspective makes life and thought stale. Insight can lead us to a non-locality and non-fixity of views, and we will find the mind has the ability to move with agility among perspectives, and not become flustered or fearful.

Basically, as soon as you are bogged down in seeing and experiencing from one position (including this one!), you are impoverishing and limiting your experience of truth and reality. Moments of insight, wisdom and genius are not miraculous castles of neural structure that just construct themselves from nothing. Rather, the artist or holy person who experiences insight or genius is subject to a differential, a movement. These people are usually paying attention and are articulate, and when their minds shift, they are able to describe the change that occurs; they *experience* the rippling of a wake behind a moving boat, or the buffet of air as a train passes. The great works of religion and art are not creative, but descriptive. Creation has already occurred. Such artists and saints are present at junctions and differentials in the flow of reality and they describe them. Shakespeare didn't create Hamlet, he experienced then described the experience of Hamlet. His mind took him to the place where Hamlet is, and he described what it was like to be Hamlet. His mind took him to a place in reality called King Lear, and he described what it was like to be King Lear. Buddha's mind took him to ultimate reality, and he described what existence looked like from there. What these people have in common, more than innate super-intelligence, is fluidity and non-fixity of mind, combined with the vocabulary, intellect, and inclination to describe the places their minds take them. A fluid mind is a limitless mind, and that is why it is so astonishing to us observing from a fixed point that they are able to observe and describe reality with such beauty and depth.

Most of us, normally, occupy the role of the watcher who is watching, and this is an impoverishment. When we have a perspective—any perspective—it concretizes us in that limited vantage, and it fixes us as the watcher, reinforces the concept of a separate and distinct ego, and sets up a false duality between watcher and watched. Releasing attachment to perspective, or views, unchains our experience from identity, culture, dogma, prejudice, and allows our experience to merge with what is, to the extinction of ego.

Let's say you are in the mountains, sitting by a mountain stream. You're looking at the water and hearing it move over rocks and pebbles. The typical view is that you are different from the stream. You are your body, your sense organs, and you perceive the stream with your eyes and ears. I suggest the conception you have of yourself as being separate and other from the stream is false, based on a false assumption, and we can trace the origin of the assumption to a restricted view reinforced by the unhealthy habit of hiding in a separate self. Yes, I know, the knee-jerk response to this suggestion is that you end at physical limits of your physical body, everything inside your skin is you and everything outside your skin is the outside world. But let's examine this assumption for a moment. Seeing and hearing the stream is a part of the experience of being you, just as much as your experience of having a physical body is. Yes, the mountain stream is there, and you are on its banks. Yes, in a way, you are separate from it. But in another way, the stream and your body are continuous with each other: both comprise your experience of being alive. There is total unity and continuity between the stream and your body, among the sky and earth, what you are conscious of, what you are not; your experience of all of it, of everything, is a continuous, unified fabric.

Now, this unity is basic Buddhism, and nothing new. The applicability to our discussion is that within this unity of person, body, senses, stream and mountain, we carve off a section to call our 'self', attachment to which is what limits our view and our ability to interact with the world. Letting go of the concept of self, and the restrictions that accompany it, is what finally permits us to connect with our surroundings in a meaningful manner. Paradoxically, with this new perspective, we become more respectful of and compassionate towards ourselves, insofar as we exist as human beings on Earth.

Turning towards your fear with love and gratitude will guide you to insight, wisdom, and ultimately back to life. We tend to think of insight and wisdom as remote and inaccessible, and when we achieve them we think we should put them in a case or on a shelf. However, when we come near truth, it simply meets you, makes your world new.

The trick, then, is to turn towards your fears and serenely enter them. There are things in the world that you are afraid of, but fear, unassigned, exists first and finds these objects in your life to live in. If you're afraid of snakes, fear of snakes is just a costume that fear is wearing. If you're afraid of making a wrong choice, fear of making a wrong choice is a costume that fear is wearing. Fear is the real problem, not the object of the fear. Fear itself is the cause of suffering and disruption, not the objects of the fear. Fear clothes itself in various disguises. It wears so many disguises to sneak and dance into your life that it can take over your conscious attention and hold you in its trance for your entire life. But if you don't reject and avoid fear, and are just grateful for it and enter it, your fearful experience will be transformed into an experience of wisdom and peace. You can now participate in life as a free person.

Stepping into the void

Looking with compassion and openness towards your fears causes an earthquake in your ground. There's a seismic shift in the way you experience you. This is not subtle, it is radical. It does not improve you, it creates a new you. I mean this in an absolute sense —the more complete your acceptance of fear and trouble, the more complete the renovation of your identity. This process, however, which could span 5 seconds or 5 lifetimes, does uncover a considerable difficulty: our tendency to cling, in this case to fear. Although we may avoid the object of our fears to a completely pathological extent, we cling to the fear itself as a matter of familiarity and perverse comfort. Even once the object of fear has been confronted, the old fault lines of fear still have a tendency to linger, out of sheer habit, although now perhaps devoid of emotional impact.

This looking at and accepting fear is a brutal, real, and *available* process. Renovating your self is not self-help or self-improvement. You are self-*becoming*. The condition attending this undertaking is extreme: you let go of all you cling to. However, that only seems extreme and brutal on this side of the letting go. On the other side of the release, you realize that the fears were lying to you and believing them you were imprisoning yourself. Really, only our habit of believing the lies holds us back. Letting go never causes anything truly bad to happen, but instead unleashes magic.

This is all very well, you might think, but how do I actually do this? How do I implement this in my life?

Approaching compassion and openness as something to *do*, perhaps on a Tuesday afternoon, will undermine your possibility for succeeding. Essentially, openness is not something to do. Openness is *not doing.* You need to be watchful for the opportunity to do nothing. Compassion and openness do take attention. When you start to get afraid or panicky, when things are spinning out of control or when they already have spun out of control, that is a very special moment. Do you know what it's like to peel the backing off a sticker? It's very difficult to find the little open corner to put your fingernail under. It looks like there's just one layer, because the sticker and the backing are so close together. You know that moment? You wonder if there even *is* a backing. But then you bend and manipulate the sticker, get a fingernail between the two corners, and separate them. So, with compassion and openness and fear, what are we actually separating here? We are separating the emotional noise from what is actually going on. The moment you notice you are becoming afraid or panicky and stop spinning and escalating is the moment you have your nail between the corners. You thought that emotions and events were unified, but they are not. Emotions colour and warp events into your experience of reality. It is a huge relief to discover that you can separate the sticker from the backing. Once you have identified that you are experiencing fear/anxiety/panic, you have nothing to do but breathe, observe, and embrace the *entire* situation. Now you are pulling the sticker off the backing. You realize minutes, hours, and days later, that the pain of previous similar situations was due to you believing in your emotional interpretation of events; that this was the whole story. Now you realize that the reality of the situation included the colour and content of your emotions sticking to it; your experience was warped because you only realized a fraction of the story—the pushy, splashy and vivid version of the story that emotions thrust upon you. As you become more accustomed to this distance between you and events, you realize how unhelpful your emotion layer has been, and you opt to make decisions and live your life without being unduly guided by its input.

Maybe because we are not things, but processes, the emotions keep coming. That is why we can't just decide once and for all to be free of our fears. We need to cultivate and keep reinforcing a new approach, a new attitude. We are dynamic beings, pitching and rolling on the ship of life, and we need the wisdom that was so painful to earn to stick with us and inform how we deal with each new difficult, and beautiful, situation. We inherited and accrued habits in ignorance; now we shall replace them with habits born of insight and intelligence.

If losing ignorance were easy or obvious, we would already have done it. It is, of course, neither easy nor obvious. Your commitment must be absolute, and you must bring to bear every crackling neuron of intelligence and attention. The temptation to slip back into old habits is strong and ever present; it takes real resolution to say 'No, thank you' to the comfort of old fears and patterns. It may take a crisis, an illness, or a loss, to sufficiently shake us out of inaction. The conviction that everything on this side of letting go can be let go of is hard won, but there must be conviction.

What, ultimately, does it take, then, to step into the void? What do you need to have suffered? What do you need to have learned? I think it merely takes a decision. You decide to believe in and act on what your heart whispers to you. You decide to reject those impulses and feelings that bear the stamp of falseness, fear, evil. In the second following that decision, fear has no power. Instead of anger, your instinct is for compassion. You follow your heart instead of your eyes or your logic. You acknowledge everything that you see and know, everything that you understand and think you understand. You see how all of this falls woefully short of the big picture. Every preference is unnecessary, every conviction a mere scrap of the great fabric of truth. Desires will never be attained, fears have already hit their mark. You realize that everything is mind, and then realize that there is no such thing as mind. You hold with each fear. Hold on to it for dear life. Embrace it, melt into it, and at that moment, filled with love for your fear, suddenly you're awake.

Printed in Great Britain
by Amazon